TOR

—————— ✦✦✦✦ ——————

*Remaining Anonymous on the Dark
Net in an Era of NSA Spying*

By Miles Price

Table of Contents

Introduction...1

Chapter 1: TOR vs. VPN...3

What is TOR (Transmission Control Protocol)?...............3

What Is VPN?..4

How does VPN work? 5

    Benefits of using TOR 6

    Disadvantages of using TOR....................................6

    Benefits of using VPN 6

    Disadvantages of using VPN 7

Can you use VPN and TOR at the same time? 7

Which works best for anonymity? 7

Conclusion 8

Chapter 2: Why Does the Deep Web Exist and what are the Secrets That Lie within It? 9

Why does the Deep Web exist?.......................................9

Secrets of the deep web...10

    It isn't as harmful as it sounds..............................11

    It is always mistaken for the dark web 11

    The deep web is full of criminal activities...............12

    Not a lot of search engines can search the deep web 12

    The deep web is actually much more than the 'surface web'...13

Top 5 deep web myths..13

Chapter 3: I2P and Freenet 16

What is I2P? 16

Advantages of I2P...17
    No man in the middle attacks................................17
    Encrypted destination locations 18
    Instant P2P file sharing.....................................18

Disadvantages of I2P..19
    Relative Youth..19
    Complex installation process and usage 19
    Content on I2P network 19
    No end-to-end encryption guarantee 20

What is Freenet?..20

Chapter 4: How to Access the Deep Web?...............23

Chapter 5: How to Download TOR on MAC Computer
and Android Phone? 29

How to install TOR on Android?...................................29
    Install Orwall...29
    Install Orbot 30
    Install Orweb..30

Chapter 6: Six Different Ways Law Enforcement Can
Monitor TOR 31

1. Mapping of hidden services directory...........................31

2. Customer data monitoring 32

3. Social site monitoring...32

4. Hidden service monitoring.......................................32

5. Semantic analysis..33

6. Marketplace Profiling 33

Chapter 7: How to Legally Navigate Through
the Dark Net and Its Markets? 34

    1. Download the TOR browser and install it 35

    2. Uncensored, hidden wiki can be a good starting
    point 35

    3. Try learning more about the dark web while
    you are accessing it 36

    4. Install PGP or GGP 36

    5. Find a good dark net market: 36

    6. Register an account..37

    7. Gather some Bitcoin..37

    8. Create a bootable USB...38

    9. Set up a secure email ID 38

    10. Use multiple VPN services..38

    11. Get the deal 39

    12. Don't trust anyone..39

Chapter 8: Bitcoins and the Power of Cryptocurrencies
and Anonymity Online..40

    What are Bitcoins? 40

    Advantages of CryptoCurrency 41
        Payment freedom 41
        Control and security 41
        Transparent information...41
        Low fees..42
        Lesser risks for merchant..43

    Disadvantages of Bitcoin 43
        Lack of awareness 43
        Risk factors and volatility 43

Still in the process of development...........................44

What is CryptoCurrency? 44

Benefits and disadvantages of CryptoCurrency 45
　1. Fraud..45
　2. Instant settlement 45
　3. Free access to everyone 45
　4. Lower fees...45

Disadvantages of CryptoCurrency..................................46

Chapter 9: 10 Things You Should Know About Bitcoin
and Cryptocurrencies 47

　1. The difference between cryptocurrencies and
　digital and virtual currencies......................................47

　2. The origin of Bitcoin 48

　3. The origin of Dogecoin 48

　4. Other digital currencies 49

　5. Bitcoin regulations...49

　6. Ben Bernake's role in changing the Bitcoin game.......49

　7. How to acquire Bitcoins..50

　8. Mining for Bitcoins 51

　9. Places where you can use the Bitcoins 52

　10. The future of Bitcoins 52

Chapter 10: The Silk Road Story and the Man behind It 54

　The history of Silk Road..55

　Arrest of Ross Ulbricht 55

Conclusion 57

Introduction

Thank you for choosing this book, '*TOR - Remaining Anonymous on The Dark Net in an Era of NSA Spying.*'

Are you the curious one who wants to know everything that happens on the dark web? It's human nature to want to find out more about something if it appears to be mysterious. The whole concept of the Dark net is sure to be exciting as hell, but anyone who wants to access this part of the Internet needs to be extra careful.

It's the age of the Internet and almost everyone tends to get their sense of validation only if they are seen online. Some of us can't let a day go by without logging onto social media sites such Facebook, MySpace or Twitter. Due to online transactions, buying and selling of products have also been made easy.

The Internet has become a place that can offer you almost everything you need. However, what it can't provide all the time is privacy. Not a lot of us are really concerned about our privacy on the Internet, but there are some who are extremely concerned about not wanting to disclose their real identities on the Internet.

Why do they seem so worried you ask? It's because anonymity on the Internet is a topic of extreme concern. There are a lot of NSA, FBI and third party hackers who can monitor every

Introduction

activity of yours online.

When you realize how risky it is to surf the web without having your identity protected, it can overwhelm you. But don't worry. Read on to find out how we can keep our identities safe in this book.

If you are eager to know what exactly the dark web is and how it can help us protect our privacy, you may benefit a lot from this book. This eBook contains a vast amount of information, which will be enough to educate you on everything you ever wanted to know about the dark web.

If you read all the instructions given in this guide, you will be in a better position to surf the web anonymously.

Our guide offers you some tips on topics such as the TOR browser, how to use it on different devices, what I2P is as well as explaining Freenet, VPN, cryptocurrencies & Bitcoins etc. It also discusses one of the most popular dark net market platforms called the 'silk road.'

We are positive that you will enjoy reading this guide. It is a completely foolproof book that will guide you through the mysterious world of the dark web and help you access it with complete anonymity. I sincerely hope that all our readers are safely able to access absolutely anything online. Happy reading!

Chapter 1:

TOR vs. VPN

What is TOR (Transmission Control Protocol)?

So what exactly is Tor? The name may sound pretty complex but it is simply short for The Onion Router. TOR is free software that encourages anonymous communication. TOR has become increasingly popular in the last few years, especially among the young crowd. TOR is capable of channeling Internet traffic via a global network of over seven thousand plus, free of cost, relays that keep the location and the usage of the user anonymous.

This can keep you absolutely safe and prevent you from getting traced by anyone. TOR service allows its users browsing of the Internet and instant messenger chats albeit anonymously.

The thing that sets it apart from the other forms of Internet platforms is that it gives you exactly what it promises. TOR is predominantly used to keep the user identity secure and encourages them to carry on their affairs without having to worry about getting traced. Since it prevents the users from any kind of surveillance, it is regarded as one of the best confidential modes of communication.

If you notice the icon of the TOR logo, it's in the shape of an onion. This is done deliberately as the onion depicts the system quite precisely as the routing form that is done by TOR is known as onion routing. TOR was actually developed by the US Navy with an aim to be able to encrypt the data multiple times without being caught during surveillance.

Hence, TOR is considered to be one of the most secure ways of accessing the Internet without being watched. Now this, of course, lets the criminals use the Internet for unethical practices and sort of lets them get away with the crimes they commit. However, Tor, if used for the right reasons, can actually prove to be quite beneficial for civil liberties groups.

What Is VPN?

VPN is short for Virtual Private Network, which acts as a tunnel between multiple devices. VPN can be used to create a secure network that can protect data traffic using an encrypted tunnel.

Through this tunnel, all Internet packets are transmitted to their destination location in a safe manner. The VPN mechanism was initially designed to work remotely. This means, in case a company requires connecting to an employee at a far-off location, they can use the VPN mechanism to stay connected to him.

This type of innovation has specifically benefited the corporate sector in a huge way. In the past few years, the use of VPN networks has shown a remarkable increase.

How does VPN work?

Let us explain this in detail. When you want to connect to the Internet, you will need to connect to a server through your Internet service provider. This helps in allowing you to access just about any website you wish to surf. The entire Internet data traffic will pass via this server.

If you connect to a VPN server, the data traffic will then pass via the VPN tunnel, which is a completely encrypted connection. This particular network will allow you to browse freely without having your identity disclosed. Absolutely no one can sneak up on you, and this includes your Internet service provider as well.

The VPN guarantees complete anonymity by covering your original IP address with the VPN server IP address. For example, if you wish to access blocked content, you will have to choose the IP address of that particular country and you will instantly appear online. This allows you to view all types of confidential content of your home country that can't be accessed by the general public. If anyone tries to sneak up on you, all they can see is the IP address of the VPN. Your original IP address remains concealed and protects your identity from getting shared.

This is how your online activities are protected from being watched by anyone

Major differences between TOR and VPN

In order to be able to compare both the above mechanisms, we will have to go through their benefits and disadvantages.

Benefits of using TOR

- It is nearly impossible for anyone to find out which website you are surfing. It's quite foolproof that way.

- It is less likely that the government or some central authority may shut down your network.

Disadvantages of using TOR

- Browsing through TOR can be quite slow owing to the different layers of packets. Another reason could be because the data needs to pass through certain relays, thereby making the browser slow. Needless to say, it's not the best choice for streaming videos.

- The end node in the TOR network is not encrypted, and this makes it vulnerable to be exposed to the sprayers.

- Although TOR seems to be pretty secure, there are a few ISP's who have found a way to block the TOR. Thus, you can conclude that the TOR is not that safe after all.

Benefits of using VPN

- The VPN works much faster as compared to TOR as there is no other middleman that you have to deal with when it comes to the requested website except the VPN server.

- As per several researches, they have found VPN to be extremely reliable and safe when it comes to providing complete anonymity. ON the other hand, the security of the TOR network is still a bit questionable.

- Certain VPN services also provide protection against

malware in their brand new client software.

Disadvantages of using VPN

There aren't any disadvantages of using the VPN network, except the fact that a good VPN service may be slightly more expensive than you expected. If you are a little tight on your budget, you may not be easily able to buy this service. Alternatively, there is an option of acquiring free VPN services. However, it's full of annoying ads that may not allow you to browse peacefully.

Can you use VPN and TOR at the same time?

Yes. You can certainly use VPN and TOR at the same time with an aim to bring in some additional security to your network. It may be a little complex to set up these two together and will have to be done carefully. If the setup isn't done correctly, it may get you into a dangerous situation.

To start with, you can set up these two networks together in two different ways. You can try connecting the VPN and then route TOR. You can also reverse this by connecting TOR and then routing VPN. However, we highly recommend you to follow the first option, as VPN is a more trustworthy network.

Which works best for anonymity?

When it comes to confidentiality of your identity, both VPN and TOR can do a great job. Both the networks can allow bypassing of censorship without you being tracked. The only difference is that when you use TOR, you may find the browser to be a bit slow, while VPN is definitely faster and offers you better privacy and security.

VPN also provides you special malware protection software that is absent in TOR. ALSO, the end nodes in TOR remain unencrypted. This leaves a chance of your Internet packet getting intercepted by hackers. It could result in being extremely damaging for your anonymity. Now you can easily take your pick and decide which network you wish to access.

Conclusion

After considering the various advantages and disadvantages of both systems, we can safely conclude that VPN should be the preferred choice of network as compared to TOR. That's not only because the VPN is faster than TOR but it also offers better security, which is what most people are looking for. Since VPN uses a more sophisticated channel for encryption, it offers faster results than TOR. VPN can be used for viewing blocked videos and file sharing using the best anonymity protecting website.

The only downside to VPN, as mentioned earlier, is that it may cost you a little more than a normal network. But for all the services that it offers, spending a little extra money shouldn't be a hassle. We guarantee you that it will be worth every penny. However, if you happen to be a smart shopper, you can also get a VPN for a cheaper price.

Chapter 2:

Why Does the Deep Web Exist and what are the Secrets That Lie within It?

Why does the Deep Web exist?

The obvious answer to the above question is to be able to hide certain things. Now how does it help us? In numerous ways actually! To give you an example, whenever you access your Internet banking account, your details may get stored on the Internet. These details can then be accessed by anyone by simply doing a Google search.

However, your account pages are kept extremely secured with the use of the deep web. Similarly, whenever you buy something online using your credit card, the deep web can prevent your details from getting hacked by someone.

Without the deep web, the Internet would have been a very risky place. We wouldn't be able to have social networks with any privacy settings, our bank accounts could have been accessed by several people or even E-shopping wasn't possible. The deep web also helps in storing a large amount of the corporate data for several companies.

Large corporations often prefer to store their valuable data on the deep web. The deep web ensures that all their data is completely safe and secure.

A lot of us think that the deep web is not really meant for the common people. What we don't know is that each one of us accesses the deep web almost every day. We unknowingly use it for accessing our social media accounts, our bank accounts and even for e-shopping as mentioned earlier. Not only that but you are also accessing the deep web whenever you try to login to your email accounts as well.

Can you imagine accessing some valuable information through your email without the security of the deep web? We need to feel secure in order to be able to share our information on the Internet. This constant need for security from government surveillance is what gave birth to the deep web. The deep web has actually become an integral part of our lives.

Secrets of the deep web

As humans, we are extremely curious by nature. The more intimidating something sounds, the more we want to find out about it. Probably, this is the reason why we feel like exploring a mysterious channel like the deep web. Now that the deep web has become such an integral part of our daily lives, it's time to find out some hidden secrets.

No, these secrets won't make you fall off your chair but you will certainly be surprised to know them. Below is a list of some of the secrets of the deep web.

It isn't as harmful as it sounds

When you think of the 'deep web' you instantly start imagining a scene straight out of a Hollywood thriller, where the hackers use it for some dastardly acts. The deep web is absolutely in vogue and is being used in several cyber thrillers. In fact, the term 'deep web' also gets used in one of the most popular Netflix series called the 'House of Cards.'

The deep web's ever growing popularity in such dark thrillers has given it a 'dark' aura, a place where criminal activities are conducted. However, it's not always that bad. The deep web has its own mundane side too.

The bright planet founder, Mr. Mike Bergman, created the term deep web. The deep web may sound really fancy to some of us, but the truth is that many of its sites are almost defunct or even poorly indexed. The deep web also plays a role in the CAPTCHA protected passwords or subscriptions. Like the Internet in general, the deep web also suffers from network errors.

It is always mistaken for the dark web

Blame it on the similar sounding names, but a lot of people invariably confuse the deep web with the dark web. Although the deep web is simpler to understand, it is often mistaken for the more popular term, the 'dark web.' While the deep web may seem like it's difficult to find using the general online techniques, it is generally accessible.

On the other hand, the dark web may require special applications to access it. To add to the confusion between the deep web and the dark web, one such file-sharing network of the deep web, is called the dark net. It's easier to get confused between the two if you are a newbie and have no clue what either one of the terms mean. But not so much if you know the difference between the two.

The deep web is full of criminal activities

This is true to a large extent. Much of the illegal activity that happens in the world occurs under the deep web, and that's why it gets such a bad rap. This is one of the primary reasons that the deep web has come under so much scrutiny from the government. People stealing someone's credit card details, child pornography, sales of ammunition etc. are all conducted under the veil of the deep web.

This mechanism is certainly used to a plethora of illegal activities that become difficult to trace. Besides the fact that for over 10 years, the United States Navy along with the NSA has made use of the deep web to collect intelligence data, the deep web still remains a haven for all types of criminal activities.

Not a lot of search engines can search the deep web

You can't really access the deep web using just about any search engine. Not all search engines are dynamic enough to be able to make the deep web accessible to us. However, there are several specialized search engines that are capable of plumbing the depth of the deep web. Even Google's fascinating search tool known as the 'Google scholar' can help us access the deep web easily.

The deep web is actually much more than the 'surface web'

So how big really is the deep web? There's no one who knows how big it is, but as per most analysts, it is much larger than the traditionally accessible web. One such research had stated that the deep web is about 5000 times bigger as compared to the surface web. It is certainly massive when compared to the conventional web.

Typically, if you only access the web for accessing social media sites such as Twitter, you are less likely to encounter the deep web. On the other hand, if you are looking for much deeper topics such as world ammunition, you may stumble upon some useful details on the deep web. However, if you are searching for illegal activities like hiring an assassin, you are trolling some unsafe portions of the Internet and you are likely to be watched by the government agencies.

Top 5 deep web myths

1. It is a portal that contains private information that people don't want you to have

We want to say that this is 'partially' true. Yes, the deep web contains a lot of information that some people do not want you to know but it's not for the reasons you are thinking. It's not always that people use the deep web to store their private details. Many companies also use the deep web for storing some important documents or even images on their intranet. The intranet used by these companies also contains a lot of database with regards to their employees.

Chapter 2: Why Does the Deep Web Exist and what are the Secrets That Lie within It?

Now, obviously, there's a large part of this information that needs to be protected from being accessed by anyone else. However, it's not some kind of conspiracy plot that the deep web is always trying to hide. For all you know, it could be some really boring information like the database of a company that gets stored in the deep web.

2. Hidden information from search engines signals the involvement of deep web

This is absolutely false. There are so many sites that hide some kind or other of information from search engines. Now, this doesn't mean that the deep web is present each time. It's a very common thing for several search engines to hide some sort of information. In fact, there is a particular file called the robots.txt or sitemap.xml, which can restrict the search engines from looking at some information on any site.

 Restricting search engines from being able to access particular information does not necessarily mean that it's exciting, or that it's related to the deep web. Also, when a Webmaster restricts a directory, it is generally filled with a lot of techie stuff that can damage the ranking of the website. It's a part of being a responsible netizen instead of something evil. So yes, there are certain parts of the sites that can be accessed via the search engines and then there are some parts that can't. Is it deep web? Probably interesting, but not really!

3. Websites that require you to confirm that you aren't a robot must have some hidden information

False. There's no truth to this theory. There are some websites that require you to confirm that you are a human through CAPTCHA's or make you select images. But they aren't hiding something always. A lot of people seem to let their mind's wander about this one and they start assuming that there might be some conspiracy behind this.

It's a possibility that the site is being accessed by bots and they want to ensure that this is not the case. Without making you manually tick on some boxes, how is the website going to know that you are not a bot? Also, these sites make all the information available to you as soon as you tick the boxes or enter the CAPTCHA code. So you have an access to all the data the minute you confirm you are a human. That doesn't sound like such an evil thing to do, does it?

Chapter 3:

I2P and Freenet

What is I2P?

The name may sound a little weird but I2P is actually deeper than the deep web. The 12P is a software that hosts several sites that can't be accessed using Google or other such general search engines. It helps in keeping the traffic anonymous by switching it from proxy to proxy.

That's not all; each machine that uses the I2P software acts as a router, thereby helping to convert the software into a fully decentralized service. This helps in increasing the security to a large extent as the traffic is diverted to different network paths, and makes it difficult for anyone to interrupt it.

Now here's what the other side of I2P shows us. Unlike Tor, if you try browsing the Internet outside of I2P, you will find it extremely useless. The I2P software does not allow you to access sites like YouPorn, BBC or even Unicornsshitting.com anonymously. So you can't just surf these sites through I2P and expect not to get caught.

The software has been created to allow usage of 'eepsites', which are hosted within its intranet. If you try to browse anything outside the intranet, you can't expect anonymity.

Additionally, you will also need to download specialized software in order to be able to access the network. It is certainly easy to install this software but rather difficult to navigate. Also, the steeper learning curve of this software has not allowed the I2P community to grow in size since the beginning. Several creators use pseudo names to chat with each other on an IRC scene using extensions. It allows people to talk to each other without a middleman server.

These are the reasons that not a lot of people have been using this software to communicate. Needless to say, they don't make much profit.

Advantages of I2P

No man in the middle attacks

I2P uses a proxy tunnel architecture that is extremely difficult to hack. There's hardly any hacker who can get through such super tight security design. In cases of attacks, a hacker can constantly monitor the traffic to the website right through the exit node and may even try to time certain messages. Such a step is taken by the hackers to observe your pattern.

Once they figure out your pattern, it becomes easier for them to gain access to all your private details and use them to their advantage. Owing to the powerful tunnel encryption, and the capacity to customize tunnel length, the hacker is unable to create any patterns. This makes your identity foolproof.

In the man in the middle attack strategy, the hacker acts as a legitimate user. As soon as a message is received, the hacker starts encrypting the data and quickly passes it on to another destination.

Now the I2P's garlic routing messages can make it nearly impossible for the hacker to decipher as compared to TOR messages. Since I2P is a peer-to-peer network, the traffic on it can get spread out on different network paths, and this is exactly what stops the man in the middle attacks.

Encrypted destination locations

Now, what are destination locations? Any type of service or eepsite that can be found on the I2P network is known as the destination. These destinations contain a 516-byte crypto key, which in turn has a 256-byte public key, along with a 128-byte signing key as well as a null certificate. Such sort of encryption is not easy to decipher.

For encryption, the routers make use of both the internal and the external file hosts. These are then stored in an address book under a particular naming mechanism that is similar to conventional DNS. All this results in a powerfully encrypted destination, which is completely decoupled by the publisher.

Instant P2P file sharing

The unilateral proxy tunnels of the I2P promote instant P2P file sharing, unlike the TOR circuits. This is one of the biggest advantages of using an I2P network. Some of 12P's services such as Tracker2.postman.i2p have grown increasingly popular for the same reasons. Both these services feature thousands of torrents that can be easily stored on your torrent client and be kept secure.

Disadvantages of I2P

Relative Youth

As compared to TOR or Freenet, the I2P network does not have a large user base, funds or even the documentation levels. This clearly indicates that I2P suffers from reliability and implementation problems. Another fact about the network is that it has been unable to reach even 1.0 releases in the past couple of years.

Complex installation process and usage

Using I2P is really not that simple. Needless to say, it is not meant for general computer users. This system works effectively on the Linux operating system. The windows or MAC are too easy to track regardless of the type of network they are using. The installation, as well as the download procedure of the I2P, is slightly cumbersome. The browsers, if configured correctly, can work much faster in the I2P. Although all the instructions are displayed on the i2Pwebsite and this also offers a help section, a lot of people can get discouraged due to the complex installation procedure.

Content on I2P network

If a user wishes to access content on the I2P network, he/she must be first logged in to the site. So, if you are offline, your eepsite can't be found. This could be one of the biggest negatives of the I2P network. There are several anonymity networks such as the free net, which allows free access to the content even when you are not logged in.

No end-to-end encryption guarantee

If you are using a proxy server, your identity cannot be completely hidden. This obviously means that you can't access sites like YouPorn and expect to remain completely anonymous. This could discourage a large population of youngsters from using the I2P.

Besides the fact that I2P is still in the process of fixing this issue, it may take some time for it to develop. The false.i2p service, a form of the I2P service, has been growing popular day by day as it acts like an anonymity retaining browser.

What is Freenet?

Freenet is a network created with the aim of protecting your privacy as well as your freedom of expression. When it was introduced, most people from China found it a useful way of acquiring information that was restricted. Using Freenet, one can publish images, songs, videos, documents or any statistical data.

There are several social media applications that can be accessed on Freenet. These applications allow you to speak your mind and help you be yourself. They could also be used to freely express your views without revealing your identity. When you publish a specific image or a story on Freenet, you have the choice of keeping your identity separate or revealing it.

There's absolutely no censorship on what you say and how you say it. The Freenet network aims at protecting your identity by keeping your data anonymous. It prevents censorship through storage of data on different computers.

The storage capacity of Freenet is actually quite massive. It supports two kinds of operation, the 'insert' and the 'fetch' data. On inserting a file into Freenet, it starts encrypting it and later chops it up into smaller pieces and then stores these pieces throughout the network. When you insert data into Freenet and decide to share it within your friend circle, they can easily access your content regardless of whether your computer is switched on or switched off.

With Freenet, you can choose to express your views unapologetically as there are absolutely no servers to attack. Plus, you have the option to remain anonymous if you wish to do so. You no longer have to be worried about what you published or whether it was politically correct or fear that someone might get offended and claim action against you.

The encrypted files can't be decrypted by people who do not have link to the files. This means the computers that store all the data have no clue about the kind of data they are storing. This makes it easier to protect your data from being accessed by anyone who doesn't have the link. This means when another computer asks for data from your computer, it can't access it without having a link to the files in your computer.

All of us wish to express ourselves as freely as we can. But then there's a tendency to easily get offended when other people start expressing their views. By using Freenet, you can't restrict anyone's freedom of expression and no one can put a stop to yours. So, while the world is busy trying to censor almost everyone's views, Freenet allows you to express your opinions without getting scrutinized.

No one likes their opinions being censored. After all, why should someone restrict you from saying something you feel? It's difficult to wrap your head around the fact that some communities can take an objection over the most trivial statements.

It's like saying you are not allowed to think or say something if it's not politically correct and acceptable to everyone. For over 15 years, the Freenet community has been uniting in higher privacy, anti-censorship properties along with decentralization to maintain human liberation. This project has made a large difference to society in several ways.

Chapter 4:

How to Access the Deep Web?

The steps to access the deep web are as below:

Step 1

For starters, you will have to get yourself a VPN (virtual private network). Yes, when accessing the deep web, you should always be using a VPN, regardless of whether you are using TOR or not. You should do a Google search to find out the best-reviewed sites for the use of VPN's.

If you are going to be using the deep web, you will have to take every care that your identity remains anonymous. You need to take your anonymity completely seriously, especially if you plan on viewing the dark net markets. If you assume that law enforcement won't try to track people who use TOR for accessing the dark web, you will only end up making a fool of yourself.

The ISP's and law enforcement are really good at tracking your identity and you don't want to make it easy for them.

All you need to do is use a simple VPN app in order to hide all your deep web activities from government agencies. Your entire Internet usage will get encrypted through the app and you will remain anonymous. You can't be traced by anyone at all, and that includes the dark net markets.

The best part of using a VPN is that it also provides you with a fake IP address. This helps in further protecting your anonymity as the fake IP address can lead the trace back to some other computer or region. Additionally, VPPN also protects your photos and private data from being hacked by hackers.

Find a good VPN for yourself, which doesn't keep any logs, offers a fast performance, is compatible with TOR and can easily kill DNS leaks. Installing the VPN can usually be done by just one or two clicks and then turning it on.

Step 2

It's not possible to use the deep web using a common browser such as the Google Chrome. In order to access the deep web, you will have to download the TOR browser bundle. Another thing that you need to remember is not to buy the TOR browser from anywhere else except the official TOR website. It's only through the TOR's official website that you can download an authentic version.

The next step is to close all other browsing windows along with apps that connect to the Internet such as Skype, Google drive or iCloud. Now open the VPN and try connecting it to a different location than your current location. You also need to ensure that you only make use of the OPEN VPN protocol since it's considered to be the most secure. Here's the official website of TOR.

https://www.torproject.org/download/download.html

Step 3

Now that you have connected the VPN, it's time to install the TOR browser bundle on your desktop or MAC. Wait until the download is complete. Once done, you need to double-click the file that was downloaded and pick a destination folder for the same. The destination folder is the one where you wish to extract the TOR browser. Now select extract and save the file.

Step 4

Now start the TOR browser by double clicking on it. Pick the folder where the TOR browser is extracted and then click twice on 'start TOR browser.' Once you do this, the TOR home page will appear in a browser window. Now that you are done, you can be rest assured that your anonymity will be protected.

You can also try gaining access to some onion websites using the deep web browser you just opened. You may want to have some fun by logging into a dark website. Since you now have the access to the dark net, you can look for the DARK NET market list and pick some of the best black market sites on the deep web.

In case you are eager to browse some dark net markets, just follow their step by step instructions with regards to sign up, browsing etc. Now that you have gained access to the deep web, we want you to remember certain points.

Step 5

Remember to make sure that you do not make any changes to the window size of the TOR browser unless you wish to risk your identity. Changing the TOR browsing window size may make it easier for the FEDS to track you down. They have programs that can easily match different identities with some random things like your online login time or the browser window size. So the next time, you get tempted to change the browser window size, you may want to keep this in mind.

Step 6

This one may come as a surprise to many. Just because you are accessing the web through TOR, it doesn't mean that you may remain 100 % anonymous. For that, you will need to manually select the option, 'turn off JavaScript' from the settings section of the browser. Without selecting this option, your identity may not be completely safe even though you are accessing the TOR browser.

Step 7

The next step will be to save your webcam from getting hacked. Don't believe this happens? Well, let's just say that this happens a lot. There are expert hackers in the market and even some government agencies that can use various ways to hack into your computer while trying to turn on the video cameras.

You won't even know that you are being watched through the camera. You may end up having some of your intimate images being used by the hackers for extortion. Not only can that but, in all probability, even the FEDS use your images. To avoid this, you will need to completely disconnect your webcam or you can also cover the camera using some black tape.

Step 8

Similarly, disconnect your microphone or you can also use some black tape to cover it. Just like the camera, the hackers can also use your recordings to blackmail you. The last thing you want is to give any chances to someone to listen to some incriminating things said in your house.

You don't want to leave any chance of any such instances occurring open to that possibility. One has to take extra precaution to ensure that they don't get into trouble by this means. And it's not only while using the deep web, but you should be doing these things while surfing social media sites such as Facebook too.

Step 9

Do you use your real name; email ID, photos or password while you are accessing the dark web? If your answer is yes, don't ever do it again. It's important for you to realize the gravity of doing something like this. Using your real identities, image or passwords can get you tracked faster than you think. You may be unknowingly handing over your personal data for the hackers to use against you.

The smart thing to do would be to use aliases or anonymous email ID's, which have no connection to you whatsoever. This is one of the best ways of keeping someone from accessing your actual information.

Step 10

Now the last step is to be aware of what you are viewing on the dark web. If you generally keep looking at some valuable information other than browsing your favorite nail color, you need to be careful of your identity. If you read this entire guide carefully, you will no longer have to worry about being tracked while accessing the deep web.

If you have read through the above points and thought to yourself 'I didn't know any of this before,' you need to seriously spend some time in assessing whether you are aware of all the precautions to be taken while surfing the deep web, and then proceed.

Chapter 4: How to Access the Deep Web?

You are probably a newbie who may not be ready just yet to start accessing the deep web. You may also want to share the above tips with your friends to avoid them from being watched while accessing the web.

Chapter 5:

How to Download TOR on MAC Computer and Android Phone?

1. Start by logging on to https://www.torproject.org/ and download the TOR browser.

2. Once you download the browser, look for TOR icon.

3. Now double click the TOR browser.

4. Click connect (It should not take more than a few seconds to connect to the TOR network)

5. Once the TOR browser pops up, you can sign up for an account and start browsing the dark web market.

How to install TOR on Android?

Install Orwall

Orwall is a firewall for android phones, which will make all the apps on your phone use the TOR network. In case the app is incapable of using the TOR for accessing the Internet, the data connection will automatically be blocked. Post installation of the APK, you can try setting up the wizard and later reboot your phone for activation of the background process.

Install Orbot

Orbot acts as a connector between the phone and the TOR network. It encourages data transmission from the apps to the TOR network. However, it can only be possible with apps that allow data sent through a proxy server. This limitation makes it vital to have the Orwall, as well as the Orbot, installed on your phone.

Installing these devices will help in connecting to apps that do not have proxy servers supporting them. After completing the setup wizard, one has to press the power button for long enough to activate the Orbot.

Install Orweb

Orbot promotes connection to TOR, whereas Orweb allows you to use TOR for surfing the web. Now your data will be going through several international TOR servers, and this can make the TOR network slower. But that shouldn't be a problem, as it's a small price to pay for the anonymity it offers. Through Orweb, you can bypass a lot of network restrictions.

Chapter 6:

Six Different Ways Law Enforcement Can Monitor TOR

Law enforcement, along with some government agencies, have been trying to crack TOR and the web crimes related to it. A particular research group has come up with a suggestion that dark net monitoring should be the top most goal of Internet governing bodies. Now there are different ways in which law enforcement tries to monitor the dark web market. All these are mentioned below.

1. Mapping of hidden services directory

TOR operates using several 'nodes' that are followed by many volunteers all across the globe. TOR smartly routes all the Internet traffic between all these nodes, which helps in anonymizing the data. If you happen to own an ample number of nodes, you can easily know more about the dark net marketplace and the people who use it and for what.

One particular report for the TOR projects indicates that about the 30,000 dark net websites don't make up more than merely 1 percent of the total traffic routed via network.

2. Customer data monitoring

Several intelligence agencies along with the NSA concluded that they could benefit a lot from monitoring customer web data to find out the links to non-standard domains. In short, the security agencies cannot only find out who and how many people are accessing the dark web but they can also create inferences from it.

This does not necessarily mean that the privacy of the people on the dark web market will be intruded upon. This is possible because only the destination locations of the web request needs monitoring without needing to look at who's using it. But then again, this all could be possible only if the intelligence agencies can do it correctly.

3. Social site monitoring

Now this may sound scary, right? Well, not really. We are not talking about social media sites like Facebook or Twitter. By social sites, we mean dark net websites. The law enforcement agencies can observe social sites such as Pastebin regularly. This is one of the darkest websites where dark web links are often updated.

4. Hidden service monitoring

Can this really be done? The answer is yes. The dark web sites invariably go offline and have a tendency to resurface too. This may make it difficult to track them. The best thing to do would be to get a screenshot of each new site, the moment it is spotted.

Once the snapshots are taken, the agencies can later monitor their online activities. Hidden service monitoring could help the intelligence agencies to a large extent in locating people who carry out criminal activities on the dark web market.

5. Semantic analysis

What is a semantic analysis? It is nothing but the study of semantics that involve the meaning of speech. Once a dark website is located, it needs to be downloaded and the information gained from it should be stored for future analysis. This can help in comparing the acquired analysis to several other hidden services to link them with malicious acts. This could be a great way of analyzing the activities that go on in the dark web market.

6. Marketplace Profiling

Creating a comprehensive database of the dark web dealers can be of great help. These dealers often keep switching between the drug markets. Their personal profiles can take some time to build.

Although there's a lot that can be done to monitor the dark web, it's not an easy process. The security agencies will have to spend a humungous amount of time trying to bring down these websites. The results will certainly show over time but it depends on whether the law enforcement of the intelligence agencies would want to spare so much time analyzing the dark web   market.

Chapter 7:

How to Legally Navigate Through the Dark Net and Its Markets?

A lot of people, mostly youngsters, don't think much of the legalities when it comes to exploring the dark net markets. Safe navigation through the dark net markets is not something any one of us should be taking lightly.

It may not seem like a big deal to you while you are accessing them, but you have no clue how you can easily become a victim of identity thefts and hacking. If you are a complete newbie, you don't just need to know how to access the dark net, but also need to be aware of how you can safely navigate through it.

The significance of maintaining your anonymity at all cost can't be undermined. If you read about some of the criminal activities that go on in the dark net markets, you will certainly vow to be extra careful the next time you access it.

We strongly recommend using the dark net markets for legitimate purposes only. Just because you have found a way to access the dark net doesn't mean you should be indulging in illegal activities and expect yourself to go scot-free.

If you do get caught violating the laws of your country, there may be some serious legal action taken against you. But we are assuming none of our readers want to put themselves through anything of that sort. So we wish to offer you some great tips for legally navigating the dark net and its markets. Read on to know more.

1. Download the TOR browser and install it

Start with downloading the TOR browser from their official site mentioned earlier in this guide. Once you download it, install the browser on your desktop. Now you can easily access the onion routing network, making it hard for third parties to trace you.

This is a good security practice to follow, as it will also prevent you from getting commercially tracked. Just running the browser won't really be enough. You will have to follow all the guidelines for online security as well as anonymity.

2. Uncensored, hidden wiki can be a good starting point

A lot of times the web addresses of the sites can change without any prior notice. This happens as these sites are often compromised by law enforcement or even hackers. Therefore, it's important to keep an eye on some of these forums online, which can help you pick the sites that are trustworthy. One such forum that can be particularly beneficial for you is Dark net markets subreddit. This forum keeps updating the latest dark net market sites that you can safely navigate.

3. Try learning more about the dark web while you are accessing it

Accessing the dark net for the first time can get a bit overwhelming. Operational security can take some time to get a hang of and it may seem bewildering initially. There's a possibility that you may be reminded of Clearnet Internet that people used to access during the mid-90s.

It is vital that you learn as much as you can about the dark net before venturing into a territory that is considered risky. Take some time out and try finding out more about the riskier sites before you login to them. You can also invest in something like Hasbro's MLP line of toys to increase your knowledge. Alternatively, you can also keep reading some informative pages such as 'how to exit the matrix' on wiki. Learning about 'security basics' could also help you to a large extent.

4. Install PGP or GGP

Installing the PGP or MGP can help you learn, create and use public or private key pairs. Once you start using the key pairs, do not ever divulge them to anyone or lose them. Avoid sharing information even with your close friends. You can try saving this information on some offline USB stick for greater safety.

5. Find a good dark net market:

This can turn into quite a task really. Finding a dark net market can take some time as they often get hunted down or hacked and hence keep changing their addresses at regular intervals. You will need to keep rechecking the addresses via different forums. You can do some Google searches and find out a list of legitimate markets.

6. Register an account

Register your own account on the dark net without using any of your real personal details. Now browse around a little to find some reputable markets that can provide enough security to their buyers and sellers. Also, you need to ensure that they have an escrow system. Having an escrow ensures that the buyers commit to a specific amount of funds upon order. At the same time, the sellers get paid only upon the delivery of the product.

Do not ever get tempted to trade an escrow system for an attractive offer or get into private negotiations. It almost never works in your favor even though it may seem like it is. This is how so many scams take place. There are certain sites on which the sellers shell out a deposit to the market.

This deposit or bond is immediately forfeited by them if they notice too many consumer complaints. Look for a site that has similar feedback systems to those of Amazon or eBay to check someone's reputation. You need to be smart while choosing a market and learn how it guards its traders.

7. Gather some Bitcoin

So now you are all set to buy your favorite pony, and it's time to shell out some money. Unfortunately, you can't use credit cards in the crypto circles as the transaction can be easily repudiated. You certainly don't want to risk your credit card details.

So how to you pay for the pony - by acquiring Bitcoin. And how do you get them? Simply start using coinbase.com or you can also pick a local exchange that will accept your currency. One particular site that is widely used and is quite trustworthy is bitx.co. Another thing that you will have to be careful about is the Bitcoin blockchain. Since it's publicly accessible, you will have to learn about how to keep your use anonymous.

8. Create a bootable USB

Spend some time creating a bootable USB with tails for using it during making actual transactions. How does that help? It can keep you safe, as it does not leave a trace on your computer.

9. Set up a secure email ID

You need to have a secure email ID with hushmail or protonmail. You are going to need this email ID during making the actual transaction. Alternatively, you can also use some throwaway addresses for conducting each transaction. Similarly, you need to look for a secure chat client such as Xchat in order to communicate with strangers. If your dark net market does not provide a secured chat facility, then you will have to use an external chat client.

10. Use multiple VPN services

It will be a smart move to use one or more VPN services. Typically, TOR is enough for operational security if you use it regularly, but it's always better to be behind multiple proxies so it becomes difficult to trace you. The VPN endpoints, as well as the proxies, are always allowed in pretty much all the liberal countries except a few.

11. Get the deal

Directly contact the seller and tell them that you wish to buy a particular Rainbow Dash toy. Once they get an order, they will ask you to deposit the payment in the market's escrow account; thereafter the product will be dispatched. Generally, the sellers use airmail to send the product overseas.

12. Don't trust anyone

Yes, trust absolutely no one when it comes to accessing the dark web. You can explore as much as you want, but make sure that you have done your homework right. All you need to do is simply go through this entire guide once to understand when and where you need to be careful. Do not share your private details with anyone on the web. Stay safe!!

Chapter 8:

Bitcoins and the Power of Cryptocurrencies and Anonymity Online

What are Bitcoins?

B itcoin is nothing but a digital currency that was created in the year 2009. It is known to offer cheap transaction fees as compared to the traditional system of exchanges. Over the past few years, Bitcoin has managed to attract a large number of buyers and sellers on the dark net market.

Not many of us know this but even though the Bitcoin address seems confidential, it may not be able to completely help you in staying anonymous. The public ledger allows the linkage of a current transaction to the previous one that originates from the same address. There are numerous approaches that one can use albeit independently or even in a combined fashion.

This helps in tracking the original sender or receiver of a major portion of Bitcoin transactions. A few of the methods that can be used for these purposes are Analysis of the Transaction Chain (ATC), mapping of the IP address, amount & taint analysis and time sequencing.

Advantages of CryptoCurrency

Payment freedom

- You can use Bitcoin to send money almost anywhere across the globe at any time.

- You don't have to bother yourself with rescheduling due to bank holidays or even crossing borders for that matter.

- You control every bit of money using Bitcoin without having any central authority figure trying to control it.

Control and security

- Allows its users to control their transactions. This helps in keeping the Bitcoin safe.

- Merchants are not allowed to charge any extra fees unless they have the consumer's permission with regards to the same.

- Since all the personal details are kept hidden, transactions using Bitcoin are considered very safe.

- Bitcoin can easily be encrypted for ensuring better safety of your money.

- Payments using Bitcoin can be made without tying your personal information with the transactions.

Transparent information

- Each and every transaction made using Bitcoin is

available publicly for all to see. However, your personal details remain hidden, so you don't have to worry about anonymity.

- Even though everyone can see your public address, your personal details are not linked to it.

- Anyone can verify their transactions using the Bitcoin blockchain at any time.

- The Bitcoin protocol is so foolproof that it doesn't leave a chance for manipulation by any type of organization or even the government. This is because Bitcoin is cryptographically very secure.

Low fees

- You won't be charged anything currently on your Bitcoin payments. Even if there is a fee, it will be very minimal. You don't have to worry about drilling a hole into your pockets.

- Whenever a user is doing a transaction, he/she might add some kind of fees for processing the transactions a bit faster. So if someone is charging higher fees, that network gets more priority and the transactions get processed much faster.

- Digital currency exchanges aid in processing merchant transactions through conversion of Bitcoins into fiat currency. Such services make the transaction process faster and charge lower fees as compared to PayPal or credit cards.

Lesser risks for merchant

- Since Bitcoin transactions are irreversible, carry no personal details, and are highly secure, the merchants get better protection from any potential losses through frauds.

- Using Bitcoins, the merchants are able to do business even on networks where the crime rate is high. The primary reason for this is because it's near impossible to cheat anyone using Bitcoin owing to the public ledger, also known as the block chain.

Disadvantages of Bitcoin

Lack of awareness

- A lot of people are unaware of Bitcoins

- A lot of businesses allow Bitcoin transactions owing to its several advantages, but the number is comparatively low.

- The workers should also be made aware of how Bitcoins work so they can help the consumers.

Risk factors and volatility

- Bitcoin can be volatile because of the limited number of coins and their demand being increasingly higher with each passing day.

- The prices of Bitcoins are fluctuating depending upon the current events with regards to digital currencies.

- If more and more businesses start accepting Bitcoins, they will be priced relatively cheaper.

Still in the process of development

- Bitcoin is still developing and has incomplete features that need to be developed

- In order to make digital currency more accessible, certain additional features and tools are being developed.

- Bitcoin may take some time before its full potential is explored.

What is CryptoCurrency?

The absence of complete anonymity is what Bitcoin lacks and this is what gave birth to cryptocurrencies. The cryptocurrencies are known to offer complete anonymity to the buyers and sellers. A CryptoCurrency is basically a virtual currency, which offers complete security through the use of cryptography.

Does that mean that cryptocurrencies can't be tracked down at all? Absolutely! Owing to the super security feature that the cryptocurrencies use, it near impossible to counterfeit them. The organic nature of the CryptoCurrency is inarguably one of its best features. By this, we mean that it's not something that is issued by a central authority hence making it completely secured from any form of manipulation or even government interference.

Benefits and disadvantages of CryptoCurrency

1. Fraud

Cryptocurrencies are totally digital and extremely difficult to counterfeit. Its security features cannot be easily reversed by the sender, even in case of credit card charge backs.

2. Instant settlement

When you are trying to buy some real property, there are a few hassles you have to deal with such as lawyer fees, delays or even notary fees. On the other hand, CryptoCurrency is almost like a huge property rights database. Bitcoins contracts are created to add or eliminate third party approval or even for using referenced external facts.

3. Free access to everyone

Almost anyone and everyone can access the CryptoCurrency. Out of the 2 billion people who regularly use the Internet, not many are able to access the traditional exchange systems. This particular group of individuals is a primary consumer of cryptocurrencies.

A particular mobile-based money transfer system by Kenya's M-PESA system has announced a Bitcoin mechanism, which is owned by at least one in three Kenyans.

4. Lower fees

Typically, there are no fees charged for CryptoCurrency

transactions as the miners get their compensation through the network. In spite of being charged no fees at all, some users engage in third party services like Coinbase for maintaining their own Bitcoin wallets. Such services work pretty much like how PayPal works while dealing in cash or credit cards.

They offer an online Bitcoin exchange system and may charge some fees. However, it's puzzling to note that PayPal does not allow Bitcoin transactions.

Disadvantages of CryptoCurrency

- Unfortunately, there are many people who don't know what CryptoCurrency is, and hence don't use it.

- There is lack of awareness in people about how CryptoCurrency can make their life easier.

- Not a lot of businesses are accepting of the CryptoCurrency.

- The sign-up procedure is a bit complicated and takes time.

Chapter 9:

10 Things You Should Know About Bitcoin and Cryptocurrencies

1. The difference between cryptocurrencies and digital and virtual currencies

Virtual currency can be termed as unregulated digital money that is controlled by the developers and accepted by people who belong to a specific virtual community. Virtual currency was created owing to the trust issues with some financial institutions as well as the digital transactions. Although virtual currency isn't 'real money,' they do not depend on the traditional banks and therefore, could pose a threat to them.

Digital currency is nothing but a form of virtual currency that is digitally stored. Most of the digital currencies are actually cryptocurrencies, except a few.

CryptoCurrency, on the other hand, can be defined as a kind of a digital currency that is extremely difficult to forfeit due to its use of cryptography. Additionally, these currencies are not controlled by any central authority, and that can be plus in terms of maintaining security.

2. The origin of Bitcoin

Bitcoin found a mention in a paper written by a programmer who operated under the pseudo name 'Satoshi Nakamotoi.' In the year 2009, a software was launched that designed the first Bitcoin network as well as CryptoCurrency.

The very concept of Bitcoins came into existence in order to take the control out of the hands of the government as well as central bankers and give it to the people. Currently, over 12 million Bitcoins are in circulation in the market. When Bitcoins were first created, the programmer had claimed that about 21 million Bitcoins were in circulation. The current value of the Bitcoins is about $460 each as per the Bitcoin charts.

The value has even exceeded $1000 per Bitcoin in recent years.

3. The origin of Dogecoin

Dogecoin is a type of CryptoCurrency that was designed in the year 2013. It was originally created by a programmer called Billy Markus from Oregon whose aim was to reach a broader demographic. In the year 2014, when the Jamaican Bobsled team could not attend the winter Olympics, the Dogecoin community managed to raise the funds for them.

The same community had also raised about 67.8 million coins so they could sponsor the NASCAR driver, Josh Wise.

4. Other digital currencies

There are several other types of digital currencies that we haven't heard much of. One of the most popular types of digital currency is Litecoin. Litecoin is accepted only by some of the retailers in the market. It is almost similar to the Bitcoin and was designed with the aim of enhancing the Bitcoin through the use of open source design.

The other types of currencies include Ripple, Peercoin, Namecoin and Mastercoin. All these are types of cryptocurrencies that generally bare the flack, as they seem to replicate other versions and offer no real improvements.

5. Bitcoin regulations

The Bitcoin currency is decentralized; however, the legalities of each country are completely different from one another. The law enforcement or even the tax authorities have been showing some serious concern over this CryptoCurrency owing to its extremely confidential nature and it being used for several illegal activities.

Bitcoin was also a primary currency used on the Silk Road, a platform that is used for the transaction of illegal drugs. The Silk Road was later shut down by the FBI. In 2013, the financial crimes enforcement network had published some of the virtual currency guidelines.

6. Ben Bernake's role in changing the Bitcoin game

Federal Reserve chairman, Ben Barnake, has played a major

role in redefining the Bitcoin game. He assured the people of America in a letter he wrote to the US senators, that Bitcoins hold a long-term promise of creating a faster and more secure mode of payment. After this news broke, the Bitcoin, which was valued at $13, suddenly jumped in value.

7. How to acquire Bitcoins

There are about three different ways you can acquire the Bitcoins, and they are all pretty easy. You can buy them on an exchange, such as the Coinbase, barter them for offering products and services or even mine them. Although the mining part is not easy, the first two options are extremely feasible. For starters, you can download a Bitcoin wallet from their official site on your PC or MAC.

There are several websites through which you can download the Bitcoin app on phone as well. Downloading this app is really simple and doesn't take much of your time. In order for you to store the Bitcoins, you may choose from the following options.

- Desktop Bitcoin wallets: These can allow you to protect your currency and do your backups.

- Mobile wallets: These can encourage you to travel along with your Bitcoins anywhere, but you remain responsible for them. Mobile Bitcoins apps also allow you QR code scanning and a simple tap for the payment.

- Web wallets: These ones can be transacted via third party service providers. However, under the circumstance that the site gets hacked, you can end up losing the Bitcoins. Hence, additional backups, as well as secure passwords, are always preferred.

Another major problem is that Bitcoins can be easily stolen in large quantities without any centralized bank overlooking it. There's absolutely no way to recover the losses if such a thing happens. There are different kinds of Bitcoin ATM's that allow exchange of Bitcoins for flat currencies. Some of these machines are extremely expensive and range anywhere about $1000 to $5000.

8. Mining for Bitcoins

Mining for Bitcoins is almost similar to gold mining, except this happens on the computer. For this, you will require specific Bitcoin software that is free and is open source. Your desktop needs to be very powerful in order to be able to mine the Bitcoins faster.

Earlier, it was easier to mine Bitcoins and some of them even found Bitcoins worth thousands of dollars of CryptoCurrency. However, currently, the hardware to find these Bitcoins is priced very high and has made it slightly more difficult to mine them. Every single Bitcoin block chain contains about 25 Bitcoin addresses, and it can take a lot of your time to find them. So exactly how much time do you need to spend in order to acquire your own?

Well, it depends upon the powder of the hardware you are using. Besides mining can also shoot up your electricity bill and you would be able to mine only a tiny bit of it.

Over the years, there are mining pools that have been designed to tackle such problems. In fact, miners across the globe can join hands and merge the power of their computers mechanisms, and share the profits equally with the participants. One of the most popular systems is known as the Slush's pool, which gives out steady payouts instead of a lump sum.

9. Places where you can use the Bitcoins

Contrary to popular belief, there are several places where you can use the Bitcoin services or products. The list includes pretty much most big corporations, small-time retailers, bakeries and even restaurants.

Not only that but the Bitcoin currency can be also used to book a flight or buy train tickets, upgrade your dating profiles or for buying products on e-gifter or overstock.com. If you search online, you will find a comprehensive list of places that accept the Bitcoins.

10. The future of Bitcoins

The value of Bitcoins may have fluctuated a lot in the past few years, but there are still over 15 million Bitcoins in the market as per a study conducted in 2016. In 2013, a Japanese exchange called Mt.Gox ended up losing about 75,000 Bitcoins in 2014 and filed for bankruptcy.

But this is not the end of Bitcoins. Experts are hopeful about the future of Bitcoins… Some experts recommend putting a few Bitcoins aside and checking how the market prices go up in the coming few years. For all you know, these Bitcoins could turn out to be the best investment you might have made in life so far. The investors and businesses who have invested in the Bitcoins could end up making the most money.

Even though not everyone knows about Bitcoins at this moment in time, as time passes, the awareness is expected to grow too.

Chapter 10:

The Silk Road Story and the Man behind It

The Silk Road was a type of online black-market, which was used for selling illegal drugs in several countries. It was the first of its kind and was operated in the form of TOR hidden service.

The users could anonymously browse all kinds of drug related sites without any monitoring. It was launched in the year 2011 and was successfully running until 2013. Initially, it took some time for this market to pick up. They only had a few sellers to start with and not many people to buy. The new sellers would then purchase accounts via an auction.

In the year 2013, the FBI put a stop to this website and arrested the founder of this site, Ross William Ulbricht. This particular man was a quintessential con artist of sorts, as he would operate under several pseudo names, one of them bring 'dread pirate Roberts.'

It wasn't easy to track him down, as he was quite clever at hiding his identity. In November 2013, a month after the original Silk Road was shut down, Silk Road 2.0 came into existence. The same administrators who overlooked the original Silk Road ran this. Unfortunately, the FBI shut it down in November 2014. Ulbricht, the man behind the original Silk Road was convicted of a total of eight charges against him with regards to Silk Road in a Manhattan court.

He was sentenced to life imprisonment without any possibility of parole in the near future.

The history of Silk Road

Henry Farrell, who was an associate professor of international affairs and political science at George Washington University, started observing the Silk Road scam in 2015. He observed that Ulbricht had created such a marketplace so he could bypass government intervention, but later found it impossible to verify anonymous transactions.

In order to sustain a good amount of revenue each month, he increased the oversight so the transaction fees could be lower. To add more trustworthiness to such transactions, he came up with the escrow payment system along with an automated review system. The FBI stated that the original Silk Road IP address was found through some data that was leaked from its website's CAPTCHA code.

Arrest of Ross Ulbricht

Ross Ulbricht was arrested on 2nd October 2013, in Glen Park Library, San Francisco. There were several charges against him including money laundering, hacking and dealing in narcotics. He had also allegedly paid $7, 30,000 to get about 6 people killed.

The FBI had seized around 26,000 Bitcoins from different accounts of SILK road, which were worth $3.6 million in 2013.

Chapter 10: The Silk Road Story and the Man behind It

During his trial, Ulbricht confessed to have formed the Silk Road website, but he also said that some other people had started controlling it, right after he founded it.

Ulbricht was sentenced on May 29, 2015, and was made to serve five sentences, which included a life imprisonment without the possibility of parole in the near future. In 2015, the new administrators of Silk Road announced the launch of I2P with several cryptocurrencies along with some listing restrictions on the original SILK road market.

Conclusion

I want to thank you once again for taking this journey with me.

Navigating through the intriguing world of the dark web requires you to operate carefully without divulging any of your personal details. I am sure after reading this guide; a lot of you will have realized how important it is to protect our privacy while surfing online. I hope the details in this guide didn't scare you from using the Internet.

You certainly don't have much to worry about if you keep all the instructions from this book in mind. I wanted to keep the information given in the book very detailed so the next time you plan on ordering some kinky stuff for yourself from the dark net market, you will know how to be careful. Not just that but the details in the book will also save you from recklessly sharing your bank details or identification numbers online.

Until about a few years ago I wasn't really that concerned about maintaining anonymity online. It seemed harmless to share your real name, address or even bank details online without having much to worry about. Almost all of us believed that the Internet is a very safe place to venture into and thought that no one would bother tracking your activities. After all, we are commoners, rather than criminals whose activities need to be tracked. But then, there are hackers out there in the market, who do want to know your details and

Conclusion

then steal your identity or even your money. If you have never thought about the dangers of someone messing with your identity on the Internet, it's about time you gave it serious thought.

I hope you enjoyed reading this guide and good luck!

www.ingramcontent.com/pod-product-compliance
Lightning Source LLC
Chambersburg PA
CBHW070858070326
40690CB00009B/1899